THE GLAZIER'S COUNTRY

POETS OUT LOUD PRIZE WINNERS

Jennifer Clarvoe, *Invisible Tender,* 1999
Julie Sheehan, *Thaw,* 2000
Robert Thomas, *Door to Door,* 2001

Also by Janet Kaplan:
The Groundnote

THE GLAZIER'S COUNTRY

POEMS

Janet Kaplan

FORDHAM UNIVERSITY PRESS
New York
2003

Library of Congress Cataloging-in-Publication Data

Kaplan, Janet, 1958–
    The glazier's country : poems / Janet Kaplan.—1st ed.
       p.   cm.
    Includes bibliographical references.
    ISBN 0–8232–2299–3 (hc).—ISBN 0-8232-2302-7 (pbk.) (alk. paper)
    1. Jews—Europe, Eastern—Poetry.   2. Jews—Persecutions—Poetry.
   3. Europe, Eastern—Poetry.   4. Massacres—Poetry.   5. Genocide—Poetry.
   6. Pogroms—Poetry.   7. Jews—Poetry.   I. Title.
    PS3561.A5592G57   2003
    811' .54—dc22   2003015656

Printed in the United States of America
07 06 05 04 03 5 4 3 2 1
First edition

For Edith Weiss,

Les R. Lopes,

and, in memoriam,

Tuvia Victor Glazer

(1900–1979)

Poems in this manuscript first appeared, in earlier or excerpted versions, in *Barrow Street, Beloit Poetry Journal, Bridges: A Journal for Jewish Feminists and Our Friends, Cross Currents, Interim* (Vol. 21, 2002, "Terror" issue), and *Terra Incognita* (with translation into Spanish by Marta Lopez-Luaces), I thank the editors and also Molly Peacock, Martie Palar, Alison Koffler, Les R. Lopes, Alexandra van de Kamp, William Glenn, Margaret Diehl, Rachel Gallagher, Craig Gordon, Jonathan Shapiro and, in memoriam, Ann Beckerman, for their generous readings and all-around support and encouragement. Much gratitude to Freddy Garrastegui of Mega Glass in Brooklyn for sharing his knowledge of glazier's shops and tools; The Ucross Foundation in Wyoming for a two-month residency during which this work began to take shape; and my family, whose ongoing support has been vital to my endeavors. Finally, thanks in large supply go to Elisabeth Frost, Scott Hightower, Yvette Christiansë, and the editors and production staff of Poets Out Loud and Fordham University Press.

This work was supported in part by a grant from the Ludwig Vogelstein Foundation, Inc.

CONTENTS

THE GLAZIER'S COUNTRY

MATERIAL

My angry grandfather was a glazier.
He took dark elements,
put them in an oven,
made something clear.

You notice these pages are opaque
as the sand glass is made of.

Product of a man who made windows
I was supposed to let him see beyond,
offer protection
from what he saw.

The future was the object.

I wasn't supposed to stand in his light
and expect him to see

the inarticulate grains.

Heat-blown. Nearly aflame.

RAIN

Noah the Righteous said, Before me, the flood,
and when he left the ark he declared, The flood is behind me.

But I say, I am right in the middle of the flood

– Yehuda Amichai

RAIN

As if the beginning loved us.
It did what it needed.

It couldn't have been clearer:
chalk mud blood.   I looked in.

Could I love
the indifference that made me?

The beginning was not thinking, it was
smarter than anything that raged

& how could rage
not form our first impulse,

we who love
indifference the least?

Look—
it may rain

rain may make
a difference   indifferent

rain
as if we waited

for rage to pass
& someone's theory of education

to prevent its happening again

rage
locked & hooked   gold

goldrush of shoes

one pair, wood miniature, w/red hand-touched petals

"Zakopanie" etched on the soles.

              File A: vertebrae   Drawer 7: femurs

shackle, wrought iron   egg, faux Fabergé

                    talon, *Stringiform*   figurine, Hummel

perfect place, Zakopanie, to find a wife   *perfectplace*

ribs locked &

                                   700

                                                  hooked, church-spire tangle

File B, drawer 6: molars

                                                            metacarpals & glyphs

when the settlers first came we had a big dance

                                                            430000

cowries   325   maxillae   6000000

medicine jars   3500   tea cups, Depression glass

          one menorah, Moroccan

                              10000000

saucers, crazed (as palms)

                                             one black braid

what right have you, who are my slave, to talk

                       why they're getting everything and our people aren't getting

those who have arrived would nearly all like to remain

(a song these things sang
as they emerged:

              THOU   SHALT NOT)

500000

               but we have deemed it useful to require them in a friendly way

to depart

                             120000

        (sang to her who knew
        in each flood's aftermath
        where everything was)

                            the shoes

           the shoes.

A man wrote

People of such a nature
                                                    (he means the *manipulative character*,
                                        identifies this characteristic in the perpetrators
                                                            of violence, the torturers)

have, as it were, assimilated themselves to things

                                                    Mildewed paper bags: one hundred

                                        Rows of articulates, human rachis trailing

& the victims?

                                                            These are mine

                                                        Are they yours?

                                        You never know when you'll need one

                                                        Is this your sugar bowl?

                                        Your yellow tooth severed from the jaw?

                                            Bleached gems, necklaces trailing

and whatever of the ability to love somehow survives in them
they must expend on devices

                                                    From raised arm to wood floor

when do those same characteristics
begin to define the victims?

[9]

when the settlers first came we had a big dance

0

and since any enemy of the emperor could not be right
the more brutally they treated their prisoners

0

but our martyrs for God will not
cease their prayers

0

(our mother kept a pair of miniature wooden shoes)

0

and remember, as the text makes clear
an eye for an eye

0

that warmth among people
which everyone longs for

0

the attacks the reverend called
punishment for our worldly sins

0

which everyone longs for, that warmth

0

nobody enjoys killing children
but we cannot forget

0

eventually we will have to thin out
the number living in the territories

0

(our sister collects faux Fabergé eggs
& Hummel figurines)

0

the Lord thy God hath chosen thee

the design
of text on a page

the pattern of
words & phrases
like moiré
or the surface
waves make
of a body of water

lines of text
like a series of mullion,
wooden slats
between units of a window

one glances out of
to wait for rain

the appearance
of absence
a zero's written shape

the adding up
of zeroes,

(these are mine)
0
when it rained the skeletons
would have been swept downstream,
becoming disassembled in the current
0
and finally deposited together
as a dense matter of bone
0
in a slower-moving section
of the river

a null matrix, all elements
equaling zero

or the zero
as O as plea

O please
keep desire

if for nothing else
for indifference

these are mine

you never know

then she began

two sisters a daughter

we said

wrong side

then soon

flood stained

one August

ready to speak.

she said

when you might need one

to say she'd had a husband

Enough

you're on the

if not now

the walls of the shop

water weighted

she might have been

so   shorn   of   his   own   that   learning it   takes   a

museum   she   was   told   pack   get out

fast   *fast*   one   suitcase one   wood crate I wanted

no   chain   fastened   on   my daughter   not even   if

its   links   were   gold   herein lies the danger, wrote the man

Zakopanie, Poland   perfectplace   she said   to   find   a

husband   that people refuse   to let the horror draw near

(lest they discover it in themselves?)   when a child is born   its parents

desire   long life for it & for this reason   (the same skill

at making horror?)   how   could   the child understand

what is an internment camp   (the same righteousness)   sometimes   I

wished   that   he   might   die   in infancy   & indeed

even   rebuke anyone   miniature shoes   who merely

speaks of it   depression china   they have already made of themselves

something like   age-ambered sugar bowl   often in my rage

have I made   of others   one   hundred   paper bags

or claimed   *I am the victim*   *mine are*   *the sole victims*

I would rather make of myself a thing   for this reason an elk tooth is given

            than possess   one more time

      this sight   slain   become slayer

these will last longer   than the life of a man

Should I not control my rage

and kill you & your kind.
Should my killing kind win to kill.

Should suffering
be an error of consciousness.

Should the rains begin—
Paha Sapa, the Black Hills

stream & thicken with light-brown silt
water the skylight

letting down to Earth a muddy radiance.
Should the Hudson overflow

to the collector's door
cars restaurants cable-boxes rushing past

a thousand teeth from a single grave
rushing past

 & the floodtide lift above Earth's sugarbowl rim
mayim hey hey hey mayim

                                              Therefore with joy

the souvenirs praising the water
that draws them forth

                                             shall ye draw water
                                   out of the wells of salvation

out of the wells of salvation.

may I not make
indifferent rain   of myself   a thing

                                          finally deposited together

waiting
for rage to pass

                                          as matter

                          not be indifferent

but with you   in difference.

                          ⅋

Define *"differ"*

                dis   *ferre*

                apart   to carry

                two   to bear

THE GLAZIER'S COUNTRY

*An efficient industry was established by Jewish glassmakers
who had emigrated from the Holy Land in the first century
in Naples, Rome, Northern Italy, southeastern France, Cologne
and other cities along the Rhine.*

— Frederic Nemberg, *Ancient Glass*

*The earliest surviving example of pictorial stained glass
is a Head of Christ from the tenth century excavated from
Lorsch Abbey in Germany.*

— Shannon Fitzgerald, *History of Stained Glass*

PROMISED LAND

A hostile climate
means a need for windows

it's 5 AM

you fill cutter chambers

                                        kerosene for a smooth run
                                              along the glass

& *snap*

A certain wealth

                        "Is the world on fire? Kinney, is the world on fire?"

                                        I don't think so

I don't think so

                & those outside are ex

                        -terior
                        -ternal

Nineteen hundred and twenty-one: Greenwood, Oklahoma

                                        No: never happened

struck from the records

                                              from the pattern

the mob heading toward the tracks.

                                           A hostile climate

I will build for you a house
I will frame for you a window

Nineteen hundred and twenty-one: toward the Golden

                                           a boy in steerage
                                           fleeing Lithuania

they were not blamed for the
Black Plagues . . . their good treatment

                                           may have been
                              because the Lithuanians were still pagans

Golden Land

                                           sun redundant above Southern heat

flames navigating floorboards

& crates marked Ample Cherries

& wagons pulling toward Negro Wall Street

                                           sailing toward the *Goldineh Medinah*:
                                           a young boy fleeing the pattern

the flames

                                           white mob heading toward the tracks.

                                           Not my house
                                           not my windows

for more than a mile a street crowded with
hotels bars jazz joints barbershops poolrooms
the premier addresses occupied by doctors dentists lawyers

                                   known as "the promised land"

                            you smear hydrofluoric acid on a rag,
                                make windows of mirrors

                                         these are
                                         hostile times

old-men bosses

                                        glass-factory fathers

5 AM

                          perhaps it is not your body

hitting her   being reduced

                                      left to rot beneath the blistering

                    to sink in the Arkansas

one hundred twenty-three

not your bodies

                                                  No. More.

∞

Better off than the *prosteh yidn*
—the "unprofitable"—

                                            your clan was better off

not until 1784 were they allowed
in any business or vocation they wished

                    few shopkeepers had panes thicker than quarter-inch
                                          in that town

possibly Mother died
before soldiers cleared it

                                          your last words for Father:

to hell with you.

∞

You who make the windows
have no time to look out

                                      leaving Lithuania: the oldest son
                                            the glazier

                    (God stays)

and my poor sister
who was two years younger than I am [said],
"Kinney, is the world on fire?"

[*20*]

I said, "I don't think so"

hallelujahs ring through the burning

        (becomes the religion continuing elsewhere)

                           no time
                        inside you
                        no desire

fleeing what was, having said

                         there was a great shadow

the woman wrote in her memoir

                         a shadow in the sky

                     plane strafing, she wrote

machine-gun fire over Greenwood, U.S.A.
a veritable capital of black economic independence

            (you prefer this inward
            silencing God the story)

(freedom, bitterly)

                     some three hundred

in the Arkansas

none back in that country

                 will you see or speak of again

the mob torching houses

as if all contact involved shattering

(& the story going silent).

Nineteen hundred and twenty-one:
Glazier,
this is the year you come sailing

not that you knew
or could care to

how a soul hardens to glass

shatters in the golden

beneath the blistering

blistering gods.

PALE OF SETTLEMENT

Broken into form by daybreak

                                             the *Forward*

the wife pouring out the grandchild's sweet flakes

                         kitchen curtains blowing back a hot breeze

the *Cherta*

                                   blue work-shirt snapped to the neck
                                          starched cuffs snapped

sugar swirls upward
in a *glezeleh tei*

Pale of Settlement

                                          sugar grain on shaved chin
                                          blackberry-brandy breath

                                          a child might think

he froze.

                              ✼

Slap of your palm: *Breakfast!*

                         Give your grandfather a goodmorning kiss
                                   She'll give me nothing

tap water sizzles in the cooking pot

                                        you have another life

                              white coinage of snow piling richly

in the here & now

the calm centrifugal center
of a subway train's ceiling fan

                          sweat of workingmen spun by overhead blades

the fan humming languages
no less foreign than theirs.

                                        Damp fingers softly grip
                                          white enameled poles

men sway, nodding awake
keeping hold the straps

                                                  clean-shaven
                                                  clean straps

clean American city   1962

                                        you remove your moist cap
                                    wipe your head, replace the cap

wicker-backed vinyl seats
the crowd of men

                                        something calm breathing:

the American not-mirror.

THE GLAZIER'S SOUL

plate glass   unscribed scrolls

the panes   must be framed   & the soul housed

else where's within   where without

to make plate glass spread liquid silica on a tray   convey & trap it

in an annealing oven   to remove the mirror from a panel of glass

pour hydrofluoric acid   over the offending image

                              it's time to discard every luxury

& so you walk home with the Sunday paper, tossing the funnies.
Amuse yourself with your children's disappointment.

die Glaser: maker of glass

for the church of Images   the stained glass Idol knows you,

        glazier   its sand origin

shimmers in your fingertips   painful to press   but the craft

you inherit then master   becomes your house

The promised kopeck: pick a fist. Which fist? Neither fist!
Then the laugh. Father's rough kiss on the forehead.
He has a schnapps. Has a name which isn't wisdom or wealth

Mr. Glazer the glazier Glazer the glazier   *glezer*   *the word "glass"*

is from zakak, *"clear." In the ancient world it was precious and so expensive*

Wisdom—where can it be found?   *neither gold nor glass*

          can be compared with it

At least I have a job! This is 1931, U.S.A. Why is she yelling? Always yelling. Warsaw
Yiddish. So you yell back. Litvak Yiddish. This is 1949. Who *speaks* to you? To whom
do you speak in 1949?

not just one who works with glass   *but someone who is himself*

transparent   *whose cardinal rule is "to be and not to hide*

the essence of being"

You, firstborn son   last in the family line of glaziers

          his fragment   his bit of glass

          the city was pure gold

                    like unto clear glass

Jerusalem

as if it was their job   the fathers whispered to you

before you fled that Europe

                                        no, we never saw it

THE GLAZIER'S DAUGHTER

Statue of Liberty the Jerusalem
imprisoned inside him

                               palms flat on the guardrail

                           sun cupped in his black fedora

the man sullen, silent

the unattainable contained
inside him

                         September sun, line of slatted seats
                                 unfolded by the rail.

He had a small shop in Brighton

                         plate glass stacked along dank walls
                                dusty sheet after sheet

                                      slit-slit-snap

discards in the corners

                                        fragments

(could his child know him, I mean his people's
names habits moods)

                               he made practical windows

                                 kept outside out

straightedge level chisels

                                    cutters smooth or notched
                                    steel-chip wheel for a blade

(his people——were they hers?)

                                    don't let your fingers near it.

Keep the poem intact

                                    I could keep it

                                imprisoned inside me
                                      an organ
                                      a sentence
                                  a finished century

                    happening again
inside me.

Sun settling on the knees of his slacks
cupped in his fedora

                            on Mother's lap a brown bag of oranges

the child's troubled
sullen, silent

Vus machs du? he calls to her
What's wrong with you?

                                        he takes the girl to see his workshop

opacity gleams in a single lightbulb's pearl

                                                        the one he's lit,
                                                        pulling a beaded chain

this is years before she learns
it was Sunday, he wasn't the boss

                                                        in corners lie fragments

(some families stayed together
inside a country)

                                                        (sometimes something
                                                            came out alive)

                        slap of his palm against the rail

                                                        Hey, what's wrong with you

Vus machs du? he calls to his daughter
slit-slit-slit

                                                        he works when they need him

                                                        his hand at her jaw

What's anyone ever done to you, skinny-as-a-noodle

idiot

                                                        slap of the wake
                                                        against the plodding boat

So leave her alone
she's at a difficult age

Mother's temper's worse than his

big flames, little flames

secrets

oranges in brown paper

fleck of his spittle
sweet as oranges

he clears a workspace on the slab

they spew their language to the salt.

&

The girl of her is his insult

hushed inside the *shul*

(the Jerusalem)

Landsman, did your wife have it?

a boy?   dead?

&

In the shop

a motor hum
& rippled line of fur

[*31*]

scrawny open-mouthed screech—

ketseleh he sings, *little cat*

unfolding a brown package

revealing a cow's heart

sweet as oranges

as secrets cupped in brown paper

(how did he get out)

(what of him survived

& – sequence –

what of herself).

&

Opaque elements made the glass

the panes
between father & daughter

intact, for now

(1946)

as if my will is what holds them

as if all contact means shattering

his fingers, nails puttied & split

                                        dig into a raw beef heart

& I could keep their suffering
at a distance

                        (inside them)

                                                their impulses
                                                behind glass

reflected in fragments

grainy in this years-later

                                        their fingers push the meat
                                        lovingly towards the mouth.

I am the little one and the grandmother feeds me.

        I don't know anything, I'm in summer school

making a butchery of math. *Why doesn't she*

        take off her shoes and count with her toes?

So I twist into myself, consider the clean floor. All those

        decent people who must have helped him

away from there, gotten him here. On television BamBam

        stronger than his parents, astronauts flown far from theirs;

Grandmother will let me watch and have ice cream

        —she'll keep the bitter man away—

when I finish throwing bones at my homework.

        My little lampshade's a carousel spun

by the heat of the bulb. At home, Mother's in her rage.

        But at my grandparent's, smiling animals ride

on smiling animals. My bed's restless passenger flies

        to Hungry Horse   Painted Desert   the stone age

the moon.

exile
astronoit: astronaut

oranges
opshtam: origin

glass
neshome: soul

a page of mathematics
psokim: verdict

Statue of Liberty
zeikind: precious infant

without gratitude
zind: sin

television
kopt'shen: smoke

Jerusalem
ainzetsen: to jail

fragmentary
farshvaigen: swallow an insult

spittle
sekunde: small unit of time

cartoon characters
tseloifen zich: run in different directions

language
zai gezunt: goodbye

restless passenger
pripet shik: hearth

carousel
tsebreklen: crumble

hunger for sweets
tsaar: grief

to exit
zain: to be

THEY

It was December & time for music

             for Teacher's spine at attention *(Venus*

in stone) fake-black hair spun ceilingward, toe-

             taps keeping time   & the tough girls

(throned cat gold calf) who'd set the high-yellow's

             'fro on fire held mimeoed sheets of Joy

thumbprinted by last year's choir   Hooky boys

             smacked handballs & curses *(thorned human)*

outside against the brick   keeping time for

             anyone fleshy glasses-bound *(a book*

of laws) or pale   At home Grandpa said *They*

      The colored   next door   upstairs   on trains   *taking*

over   *(a throw of coins)*   *(what did I owe)*

             the grapefruit sailing from dark-skinned hand for

his daughter's neck   & surely meant for her

             (what did I owe the dead & invisible

forces)   when their "doctor-king" was shot   Now

             he tossed my 45s my Rockin'

Robin my   *(what did I owe the apple core)*

             One Bad Apple   *(mushed in my lunch pail)*   He

didn't belong here   You don't belong   here

I screamed,   who'd never seen Cossack or corpse

(that thou doest)   Then   like the black girls

        I sang stanzas One   *(do quickly)*   & Two

& someone cried   *(my desire for revenge)*

        "It should say   why doesn't it say CHRIST here?"

"It should say CHRIST—"   Now they looked at the Jew—

        "Public schools won't allow this"   *(not refraining)*

said Teacher   our white teacher   "but since there's

        no one who objects—"   *(I did not refrain)*

Once, I needed to know: did she Praise Him

        for giving her an outsider   to bond her

with her difficult charges?   & what was

        IDENTITY   I was supposed to have one

(gods false alliances false self false)   say

        I was Black   *(not whole)*   I was a Jew

December   in the last

Joy   pasture

Curses   rear hoof

Pale   the face beneath it

They   nettled hands, a sign

Music   for an egg
                                                        sorrel soup

Christ   frost floors
                                                        half a loaf
                                                    one salted fish

Teacher   to rouse those not at sea
                                            to the fact of the sea

Self   spacious the sea

EIGHTEEN TREES

1.   *And when ye shall come into the land and shall plant.*

2.   For to sustain them is eternal. (As the flood is surely.)

3.   Bring water to the sand and rocky soil.

4.   Didn't the leaders say come, anyone desiring land can come.

5.   The ruins (stones hard and dry). The wailing.

6.   They saw I was a sapling, a skeleton, the survivor of skeletons,
   they wanted me to live, they said *rise again.* (Wailing
   at Europe's wall.)

7.   Who has ever wanted as little and as much as a tree?

8.   *Chai:* a gift for the living on her eighteenth birthday: eighteen trees.

9.   To sustain. To irrigate. (The rising water will not soften the wailing.)

10.   And so they planted me, a certain slenderness of torso.

11.   To make of me a State, like that of the

12.   *We are used to believe abroad that Palestine nowadays is entirely
    desolate . . . without vegetation . . . anyone desiring land there
    can come. . . . We are used to believe that Arabs are savages from
    from the desert . . .*

13.   My branches are barbed-wire beautiful. My light scatters like seeds
    onto the earth.

14.   And so they planted me and I was shot through with green.

15.   And the Nation-State spread its myth-roots (while still shot through
        with green).

16.   Does it feel eternal now, the State? The flood of suffering,
        the righteousness?

17.   Solid stone, solid as faith
        as the slowly rising walls of a flood
        slowly spreading shoots of a myth

        someone whose name wasn't Theodor Herzl
        someone less heard, read, known
        writing (in 1891)

18.   *It will grind its people's spirit in the dust.*

ON THE EVE

God decides who lives, who dies.
Grandfather snores, Grandmother sighs.

Te-ki-ah, the ram's horn intones:
Satan roams, Satan's at home.

In a bedroom, across from an el,
a flash, a spark from the third rail

lights the ceiling—femurs and ribs.
The child counts them. She's fingering

her way in, beneath her sheets,
to find the feeling, whole, complete.

Te-ki-ah! cries the horn of the ram.
Feeling, whispers strength underground.

Grandmother yawns from her twin bed.
The child longs to break the dead,

the body's table as it strains
beneath its stoic cups and plates.

Passover comes and, on the eve, wine,
spilled on the linen as they dine—

purposefully spilled but not for pleasure:
one must feel what others suffer

—exiled fathers, vengeful slaves—
at the naming of the plagues.

THE GREAT PURPOSE

My social-worker father
said he'd be all day
in the field so I pictured   *You were put*
a brick-strewn lot   *into the world*
him lost to why   *by God*   *Call the dog a doll*
they'd sent him there
but Mother stayed home
tended my bandaged knees   *easier to say*
where her coffee   *and given*
(a moment's impulse   *to us*
toward expression)
had come splashing
when she was depressed   *so that you*   *I don't*
she slept   *might grow up*   *want this doll*
or let her father in   *to be a strong*   *anymore*
Grandfather
surveying our dirt
crusts of   *say you dressed it*
smears of   *healthy and pure*
a dog's wipe in our carpet   *woman*
his insults
making them doubly ours   *in your own old*
You you you   *baby clothes*
What do you feed your child?
swearing to call   *found the twine*
an agency   *in their room*
to have me taken from you
Mother

when I was old enough
you went off to work   *a doll's eye*
briefcase full of claims
could you hear it   *can it widen*

wife & mother
Grandfather paid his token
guided me sternly
under the turnstile
& we traveled not speaking—
you had let him take me
did you know
your daughter
wished you sick
asleep or savage
but *with* me? I wished
these things for you,

below ground as I was
& headed
toward his workshop

and some day

when choking

those are your
hands
working

the twine

have children

of oh so many

of your own

moments'

expression.

When Father is studying, all must be quiet

this father from the shtetl
doesn't study

cutter in one hand, glass edge grasped with a rubber mitt

in the Great Depression

in three clean rooms

(the rooms the child's earliest recollection of her mother)

brown paper laid out on the table

for his tools

                                      they might stay rent-free
                                  here two months, there two
landlords *that* desperate

                  all must be quiet

rack to hang long johns, suspendered pants
work-boots beneath, polished

                        she remembers fingering loose the taut-tied pigtails
                                  a constantly painful scalp

                            Mother washing Father's shirts
                            Mother hunched over the sink

suds mingling with tears
the hidden tears

undershirts drying on a string

                                  the fury of those hands
                                    at her panty crotch

how she'd hunt there for urine
or worse.

         A few months here,
there   it's her job   to keep the girls from fretting
         lost friends, precious doll forgotten   late at night, his
key in the lock, sullen man   lipstick mouths on his jacket
         an American woman he'd hung mirrors for

                                              the ignorant man

is less adequate than a woman for he
has been commanded to have much learning

she is leaning thick shoulders over the sill   fix-gazed
up the side street   for the little girls to come home
          to be scrubbed

a woman is not supposed to have learning
and to the extent that she achieves it

scalps gums tongues nails anuses
          hold the napkin beneath their mouths as they chew
catch each crumb

her Jewishness may be impaired

beautiful the rooms with their airy green drapes
lace on the consoles   she was from Warsaw after all
          had brothers who'd gone to university   their dear father
waiting all those years in New York   to take the family in

now she needs her husband to return   either way she'll die
          —she knows this—
                    of the absence of a book to read
          the absence of lilacs.

Female angel of death!
(his tongue, so dramatic
it haunts, it *speaks* to her)

the father will spit
his daughter's college-going
out of his house

how could she forget

[*45*]

all he's done for her / all he's been through

it will be a good plan
for you to take up some
of the little duties around the house

she's there,
putrid in his mouth

she's at Tremont Station
textbooks in arm

the morning-bus crowds

she remembers being a girl in a blue coat
waiting for an emptier bus to board

while the glass pane between father & daughter shatters

the girl thinking: sew the third buttonhole
find a better-matching scarf
sew the buttonhole
find a scarf.

(Eighteen, I think, when she had
her first breakdown

—What do you mean, "breakdown"—

I mean they took her for electroshock
without telling her where she was going)

and make them part of your
daily work. This will take your mind
away from yourself

then the treatments to keep secret

and will, in a measure
give you some of the housekeeping knowledge
which is so necessary

the lies

the man who marries her marries these lies

to have children of your own—

—that is a woman's great purpose

of course she doesn't think
wait forty years to be a suicide

shatters, my metaphor
to keep the violent father distant

she keeps house.

(There's a photograph of her and her sister from back then—dressed alike in these Bavarian-
alps-milkmaid dresses. White collars, black bibs with red and white flowers along the hems—the photo
was tinted. Europe, for godsakes. Little soldiers. Each hair in place: banana curls for my aunt, braids
for my mother. My grandmother must have hated all that messy red hair. . . . So when Mother gave me
the book about housekeeping and "the great purpose"

—Maybe you should keep to your own childhood.—

I'd rather not.

—Why. Still afraid you might hurt something?—

Can't I protect? Haven't I said plenty, now and before?)

One day, home for lunch,
I said I'd lost my keys.
This was a slap—
Who would let me in at three?

What did I expect she'd be?
Would I trick her into playing dead?
I was not her friend, she said,
And what she'd like to do to me.

First a need for new keys cut,
To push me ten blocks there
By the nape, my hair. Then a need
To let the neighbors see.

Father wasn't home but
Social-working poorer themes.
Later we two watched crime shows
On TV.

At the Bronx apartment's rear
A room filled up with Mother's "junk"
None entered, not even she—
Pets crawled in to die. Years back

She'd left some rhyming couplets
Near a mound of high-heeled shoes:
Unfinished halves of thoughts,
The half-finished lessening

Of a great rage. . . . At seven
I was a slow learner
But I had better learn, she said.

I had better see.

How little I would have liked
To see my work: frame a view
Of that brief unredeemable
Time or be damned by it instead.

"J—

     *Your grandmother gave me this book to read when I was about 7 - 8
and I believed every word.*

—H"

(H. G. K. 1933–1991)

Don't you see? cut, polish, cut

It changes—appears changed—

Refraction of course

Why bother letting light through?

Already through—

THE GLAZIER'S NIGHT

what has a man opened
with care   with tools
0
one pane murder   one pane suicide
one pane living
(passed over, bitter, bitten into)
0
did you want to break open?
illness blows in
through a cut to a toe
0
—he might have said something when it began to hurt,
he might have told us—
0
violence against them that followed
the assassination of the Czar,
May Laws which barred them from cities
0
what has he opened?
his leg pulses in abstentia
0
I was thirteen with cramps,
not allowed on the ward
0
sweating my sundress
a blood smell
0
some 2,600,000 left those countries
0
think how recently
—ambivalently (just a girl), eagerly (you could live through her)—
your blood came here to be me
0

it's open now, it struggles

0

did you want to slide your wheeled blade
across yourself, lift out
something clear?

0

—you'll go see him,
we're sneaking you in, don't be spoiled—

0

many more stayed behind
(&, small as a toe, it began)

0

(removing a bunion, cutting a toe)

0

did something long to fly out
of you, grandfather, it flew out as you failed

0

tissue-gown slipping from your thigh:
Out—all of you

0

one pane + one pane + one pane

0

flew from the machines of health
the faithful white-clad world

0

all of you stink

0

the slavish marching steps of order

0

clear glass are you
back in the frame now are you back
among the ones you left
who didn't get out in time?

0

someone shrouds the mirrors
as if by frost

0

was your God a glazier, did He make windows?
did we gaze at one another's lives
& expect to see through?
0
You want ice cream.
Go to the cafeteria for something sweet.

MORNING SERVICE

God lists who'll live who'll die
and the year begins
He's having none of it
his name on neither list
memory the god the hell
schnapps cutter straightedge
gangrened foot
taunts to his wife grown matronly
A hand-mirror? Why don't you look in the toilet?

In the next room
the lover sleeping, sanctity of orderly breaths
I've worked when I should have slept;
ailanthus by the window murmuring,
cat asleep on papers,
5 AM

He trundles cane-first
but muscular
into the blizzard
left shoe laced to fake foot

Vu gaistu?   *Away from you!*

The wife and granddaughter: his foes in the living room
feel our lives contract   a chest pain
and he goes

Lit screen in the here and now
messy desk   murmurs in the yard
morning placed firmly
setting order
upon the day to come

upon the face
of the deep

&

Cane-first he disappears
jays nudging the linden
settling back in the lightdark
love asleep the
sanctity of orderly breaths
mirror going
to window
I should have slept

Let there be

more dark

&

Here now, an exile's face
lucent, caught
on the screen
mutable on the glass
now the softened frame of infancy
now of old age, nasal folds deep ravines

Lithuania

"Golden Land"

Away from you

&

But he turns toward me,
his foe in the living room,
turns

[55]

A hand-mirror? Go look

in the blank screen *Go look*
in the blizzard
the desert
the lightdark
turns

THE WINDOW

Out of Nebraska, endlessly rocking toward Colorado

> solitude thick as cloud cover
> as horizontal weather

black milk of daybreak

> *She was awful friendly with that Mexican guy*

Will you watch my son for me?

> *There is no good ground. Everybody out there working in a factory*
> *or something*

a woman's hand lifts a pint of milk, positions the straw

> *Put her hair on top of her head, she'll look like someone different.*
> *Give yourself a little variety, you know?*

I won't let nothing happen to your boy; I have one too

> crackling a bag of chips

Of course the train always slows in the poor neighborhoods

where in this country will I go
to add a languagelessness of miles
a measure of loneliness

> what can I know of your loneliness, forced traveler
> from Village X
> where things of no worth

                                                        must not be wasted.

Black fields ticked gold with hay

                                                        building X crop X

Seventy-four thousand dollars for eighty acres

            Last year we were hurting at seventy-two a bushel, fluctuating

That's corn, but beans were steady as can be

                        My advice? If you got crap corn, they'll take it

They'll take anything

KFC   Wise Furniture Depot
                            red corrugated roof   smattering
of red three-story bricks
                            cottonwoods   *that's a real nice stand of oak*

                                                thick as cloud cover
                                                as horizontal weather:

                                        solitude. Beside each house one lamp

shimmers green. Dirt-cuts
hidden by night   seemingly random

                            dotting of green-cast lamps along the prairie
                                                at daybreak.

On the hearth burns a fire
And indoors it's hot
And the teacher is teaching small children
The alphabet

clan with deep nasal folds with long nostrils
blue eyed pale haired straight edges muscled arms

               from Village X Father X Mother X

X *ben* X

                                    (name engraved).

∞

I arrive in high desert

                                the state least peopled

                it's April

the cut meanders grazing land, rises with the hills

                                once a vast inland sea

sage
abloom in the gumbo

                overtakes   assaults the foddered air

snow powders matted spines

             Wyoming wind tight around the throat

hillafterhill   sky   more sky

in one hour

                           a factory of seasons

distance   nearness

                                                        immeasurable.

Endless high plain beginning to green

                                              scurry of mule deer
                                              down the shadow side

                    you asked to root your life
                              —ours—
                    in this tentatively tolerant place

ring of teepee stones on a rancher's hill
quarter mile past the barbed-wire fence

                         fine; I set my view.

April

                                        Clearmont, Wyoming

bison herd tromping rain-swelled *peau-de-soie*
to hard mud

                         recovered

                                                            for especially lean meat

millennia of obscurity

then prairie grass

                                                    taller than a man for miles
                                    so thick the first to cross had to hack his path

limestone jutting black yellow black

teepee stones Martian red

                                            eventually we will have to thin out the number
                                                of Palestinians living in the territories

nameless   covered   renamed.

Ofyn pripetshik brent a fayerl,
Un in shtub iz heys.
Un der rebe lernt kleyne kinderlekh
Dem alef-beyz

                                                    this month they're born & branded

                                                    fall's castration season

Mr. Glazer the Glazier

                        Grandfather, Man-on-the-subway

shall we root ourselves in uprootedness?

                                                    there was once a vast sea

endlessly rocking

40 million years ago
it parted

                                          before me, the desert

The filmmaker went to what had been Birwe
to film Darwish's childhood landscape . . .

                                          On April 16 Israeli bulldozers
                                          began paving a new road

through the graves.

              You looked out of the subway window's open mouth

                                          siblings, parents

(about them you said
they were *lost*

birthplace   *dried up)*

                                          riding from Bronx to Brighton
                                          the ocean to see

              (you said to your granddaughter *I'll take you,*
                    come, I'll take you to see)

abandoned parachute jump jutting red yellow red
Brighton Beach stuccoed with sharp cracked shells

                                          Atlantic a bridge joining
                                          Hastened-Away-From to *Trying-to-Forget*

& in the higher elevations
limber pine & aspen

                              a factory where a Lithuanian boy cuts glass for windows

                                        (it's 5 AM)

the Bighorns catch fire

                        & light refracts
                        in a sliver of you

                                                    I'll close my eyes

                        day breaks

by an extinguished sea

                                        extinguished & therefore mine to claim
                                                            or be free of.

Az ir vet, kinder, dem goles shlepn
Oysgemutshet zayn
Zolt ir fun di oysyes koyekh shepn,
Kukt in zey arrayn

                                        Whereto answering, the sea
                                        Delaying not hurrying not
                                        Whisper'd me through the night
                                        and very plainly before daybreak

As you, children, are burdened with exile
You will be weary
From the letters you will get strength,

Look to them.

❧

I come to an *extinguishment*

> how many have come & taken shells beads stones

as if the past can redeem

> —wasn't it too set on sand?

> > it redeems
> > the way our companionship redeemed,
> > Grandfather Tuvia

past & present linked
by helplessness   pity   illusion of link

❧

fake leg & workingman's cap   padded zippered jacket

    from Bronx to Brighton   *the ocean to see*   bone-blue eye

steel hair   sandstone deepening creases   the cut meanders   from

    muscles   small fossils   to the sides of thin lips   sea beyond

history   clan with last name X   *the arid plain*

    limestone glinting   from the smashed factory   What shall I pick up from here?

Justice?   Revenge?

                                                        revenge

has ever been the window

                    & the country

                                        the glazier's country

the goal of solving this problem
has been obtained

                                        we can now report a total
                                        of 133,346 killed to date

writing not for their sake but my own

                                        I have found that the land is fragile

          salam   *shalom*

          O kin sleeping within me, at the ends of the earth: peace be unto you! Peace.

writing not for the future

                                                        but for my soul

                    as if one soul saved
                    can ever be enough.

[*65*]

On the ferry's upper deck

The sun cupped in his black fedora. A line of slatted seats unfolded by the rail. September sun settling on the knees of his slacks. *Vus machs du?* he calls.

OR, TO BE

IDENTITY

Someone wanted to know what it *felt*   *felt like*

                        condor   ponderosa pine

sun pitchering over storm clouds

to be here & now

                        to flood the metal sphere

                                        with pleasure & anthrax

          write the destabilizing formulae   & jesting antidotes

de-scribe the recording of deeds & the shedding of tears

         & to shed that   to tidy hands   in the evening tide

our doctor writing (now we are complicit)

                      from the beach house (& the satisfactions of design)

I knew the results of my studies

                could be used to kill people   *but couldn't figure out*

how to reconcile this knowledge

                        with the pleasure I derived from research.

OR, TO BE

Count from Precambrian algae

        count Joshua tree

     Cyperus papyrus   citrus & clove

   Namib darkling beetle standing on its head

          count condensation

     each drop's glide down the wax-waterproofed back

         wing cases   black legs

         at the breeze

  count thirst

count goatskin drum seasoning the land like harissa on hummus

   count Not Being & Never Was   lending their limitless lines.

The question's not answered

    without luck   hardwiring

  to bear these   & bear   even your cranky neighbor's stories

    she always chooses the expensive dish

he lives in his own world

& the stranger   (your father?)

          polishing the finials of his granite gate

          on a March day in his Florida yard

                              above the once-swamp   once-lush

     the cut orange

          yielding itself   on the glass plate

               but even this can be cohesion

          harsh cohesion.

⧉

Hardwired

     as if in your biology   & not

               any belief   is all your reason—

⧉

                                        & since

there's no Eye   to admit beholding   no Eye no

                              Cause Judge Pardoner

     tell yourself to reason   oneself's evil   oneself's good choose good

        (ah, already an exhortation

                a *coldness* that counteracts)

solo & each day

     (soul please be kind)   over faith

   over clan or country   it is an art

     & each day again.

NOTES AND SOURCES

Rain

Excerpt from the poem "The Bible and You, the Bible and You, and Other Midrashim" in *Open Closed Open* by Yehuda Amichai, translated by Chana Block and Chana Kronfeld.

when the settlers first came we had a big dance: adapted from a sentence by Manuelito (Navaho) in *Bury My Heart at Wounded Knee* by Dee Brown.

what right have you, who are my slave, to talk: adapted from a passage in *Incidents in the Life of a Slave Girl* by Harriet A. Jacobs.

why they're getting everything and our people aren't getting: from "1942: Heart Mountain: Building a Home" in *Crossing Wyoming* by David Romtvedt.

those who have arrived would nearly all like to remain but we have deemed it useful to require them in a friendly way to depart: Peter Stuyvesant, governor of New Amsterdam (letter to the colony's directors in Amsterdam).

People of such a nature have, as it were, assimilated themselves to things, and whatever of the ability to love survives in them they must expend on devices: from "Education After Auschwitz" in *Critical Models* by Theodor W. Adorno.

and since any enemy of the emperor could not be right the more brutally they treated their prisoners: from *The Other Nuremberg: The Untold Story of the Tokyo War Crimes Tribunals* by Arnold C. Brackman.

and remember, as the text makes clear, an eye for an eye: adapted from a remark by Mahmoud al-Zahar in "The Dreamer" by David Remnick. *The New Yorker*, 1/7/02.

that warmth among people which everyone longs for: George Kateb, "Undermining the Constitution." The Sixth Annual Irving Howe Memorial Lecture, City University of New York Graduate Center, 11/15/01.

[*73*]

the attacks the reverend called punishment for our worldly sins: adapted from a remark by Reverend Jerry Falwell quoted in "Occidentalism" by Ian Buruma and Avishai Margalit. *The New York Review of Books*, 1/17/02.

nobody enjoys killing children but we cannot forget: Mahmoud al-Zahar (ibid.).

eventually we will have to thin out the number [of Palestinians] living in the territories: excerpt from a sentence by Israeli Air Force Commander Eitan Ben Eliahu, in "War Butlers and Their Language" by Mourid Barghouti. *Autodafe* no. 3, 2003.

the Lord thy God hath chosen thee: Deuteronomy 7:6.

when it rained, the skeletons would have been swept downstream . . . and finally deposited together . . . in a slower-moving section of the river: description of a block of fossils from Agate Springs National Monument, Nebraska, in the American Museum of Natural History, New York.

I wanted no chain fastened on my daughter, not even if its links were gold: Harriet A. Jacobs (ibid.).

herein lies the danger . . . that people refuse to let the horror draw near [and] indeed even rebuke anyone who merely speaks of it: Theodor W. Adorno (ibid.).

when a child is born its parents desire long life for it [and] for this reason an elk tooth is given . . . these will last longer than the life of a man: Oku'te (Lakota). Exhibit catalogue, George Gustav Heye Center, New York.

Therefore with joy shall ye draw water out of the wells of salvation: Isaiah 12:3.

Promised Land

"Is the world on fire? Kinney is the world on fire?"; I don't think so; and my poor sister who was two years younger than I am [said], "Kinney, is the world on fire?" I said, "I don't think so": testimony by Kinney Booker in "Unearthing a Riot" by Brent Staples. *The New York Times Magazine*, 12/19/99.

they were not blamed for the Black Plagues . . . their good treatment may have been [because] the Lithuanians were still pagans; not until 1784 were they allowed in any business or vocation they wished: from *The Jews of Lithuania* by Masha Greenbaum.

for more than a mile a street crowded with hotels . . . known as "the promised land"; a veritable capital of black economic independence: Brent Staples (ibid.).

"there was a great shadow, a shadow in the sky": from "Events of the Tulsa Disaster" by Mary E. Jones. In Brent Staples (ibid.).

The Glazier's Soul

the word "glass" is from zakak, *"clear." In the ancient world it was precious and so expensive*: notes on Job 28, www.bible.org/netbible.

Wisdom—where can it be found? neither gold nor glass can be compared with it: Job 28:12.

not just one who works with glass but someone who is himself transparent, whose cardinal rule is "to be and not hide the essence of being": from *New Sectarianism: The Varieties of Religious-Philosophical Consciousness in Russia* by Mikhail Epstein.

the city was pure gold, like unto clear glass: Revelation 21:18.

They

that thou doest, do quickly: John 13:27.

Eighteen Trees

And when ye shall come into the land and shall plant: Leviticus 19:23.

We are used to believe abroad that Palestine nowadays is entirely desolate . . . ; It will grind its people's spirit in the dust: from the essay "Truth from Palestine" by Asher Ginzburg, who wrote under the pseudonym *Ahad-Ha'am*, "One of the People." In *Israel: Politics, Myths and*

Identity Crises by Akiva Orr. I am indebted to Tariq Ali's *The Clash of Fundamentalisms* for introducing me to this essay.

The Great Purpose

You were put into the world by God and given to us . . . and some day have children of your own; it will be a good plan for you to take up some of the little duties around the house and make them part of your daily work. This will take your mind away from yourself and will, in a measure . . . ; to have children of your own—that is a woman's great purpose: from *What a Mother Should Tell Her Little Girl* by Isabelle Thompson Smart, M.D. (ca. 1945).

when Father is studying, all must be quiet; the ignorant man is less adequate than a woman for he has been commanded to have much learning; a woman is not supposed to have learning and to the extent that she achieves it her Jewishness may be impaired: from *Life Is With People: The Culture of the Shtetl* by Mark Zborowski and Elizabeth Herzog and from its introduction by Margaret Mead.

The Glazier's Night

Facts about the Jews of Lithuania and Eastern Europe are from Masha Greenbaum (ibid.).

The Window

black milk of daybreak: from "Death Fugue" in *Poems of Paul Celan*, translated by Michael Hamburger.

On the hearth burns a fire / And indoors it's hot / And the teacher is teaching small children / The alphabet; Ofyn pripetshik brent a fayerl / Un in shtub iz heys. / Un der rebe lernt kleyne kinderlekh / Dem alef-beyz; Az ir vet, kinder, dem goles shlepn / Oysgemutshet zayn / Zolt ir fun di oysyes koyekh shepn, / Kukt in zey arrayn . . . ; As you, children, are burdened with exile / You will be weary / From the letters you will get strength, / Look to them: lyrics in English and Yiddish from "Oyfn Pripetshik" ("On the Hearth") by Mark M. Warshawsky.

eventually we will have to thin out the number of Palestinians living in the territories: Israeli Air Force commander Eitan Ben Eliahu, in "War Butlers and Their Language" by Mourid Barghouti (ibid.).

The filmmaker went to what had been Birwe to film Darwish's childhood landscape . . . ; On April 16 Israeli bulldozers began paving a new road through the graves: from the introduction, by Munir Akash and Carolyn Forché, to *Unfortunately, It Was Paradise* by Mahmoud Darwish, translated by Munir Akash and Carolyn Forché (with Sinan Antoon and Amira El-Zein).

Whereto answering, the sea / Delaying not hurrying not / Whisper'd me through the night / and very plainly before daybreak: from "Out of the Cradle Endlessly Rocking" by Walt Whitman.

the arid plain: from "The Wasteland" by T. S. Eliot.

the goal of solving this [Jewish] problem has been obtained . . . we can now report a total of 133,346 killed to date: from the 11/25/41 and 12/1/41 secret reports of Karl Jaeger, commander of the Einsatzkommando 3 in Lithuania. In Masha Greenbaum (ibid.).

I have found that the land is fragile: in *Palestine as Metaphor* by Mahmoud Darwish.

O kin sleeping within me, at the ends of the earth: peace be unto you! Peace: from the poem "On the Slope, Higher Than the Sea, They Slept" in *Unfortunately, It Was Paradise* by Mahmoud Darwish (ibid.).

Identity

I knew the results of my studies could be used to kill people but couldn't figure out how to reconcile this knowledge with the pleasure I derived from research: from *The Chilling True Story of the Largest Covert Biological Weapons Program in the World — Told from Inside by the Man Who Ran It*, by Dr. Ken Alibek.

Or, To Be owes its attempt *not* to exhort to Theodor Adorno's essay "Education After Auschwitz" (ibid.).

AFTERWORD

The poems in Janet Kaplan's *The Glazier's Country* are at once an excavation of family history and an exploration of poetic form that might bear the burden of such a history, particularly when that history is charged with a duty towards a tradition that has been subjected to a violence that sought nothing less than the destruction of an entire people. That violence was the attempt to systematically remove all Jews from Europe. That such events challenge language and demand an articulation that will never, but never, succumb to the sentimental goes without saying. What Janet Kaplan's book has achieved is not only an exploration of how one lives with someone who has survived atrocity, but how an entire family or people might live in an elsewhere which demands allegiances to its now and here. In form, the book's scope is never allowed to dwarf the delicate traversal of familiar relations, filled as they are with baggage. Thus, where the book spans generations and continents, disasters and private victories, moving geographically from the specter of internment camps in Europe to sailing into a country that lies in the shadow of the Statue of Liberty, the poems themselves travel across the page with an exquisite sense of the line that must always remain strong enough to bear the weight of responsibility, but thin enough to resist any language that might distort. At the heart of this book, one generation is the shard that falls from another, into a new country, only to be haunted by the old, both fretting against the clear glass that is at once the surface of the poem and its framing device. In this, Janet Kaplan's achievement is to tell us how we might live with history's most inescapable legacy—the fragment. A man, the poet's grandfather, who is the sullen, demanding, tender counter force to the poet's own perplexed and vexed scrutiny, can only be viewed from the distance of time and experience. He is the glazier who "makes practical windows / to keep outside out." But glass, as Kaplan shows, is a strange substance, and what is outside slips through into the imagination, making its own home there, strangely familiar, frighteningly, beautiful and irresistible—like this book itself.

Yvette Christiansë
August 2003

Janet Kaplan's first book of poetry, *The Groundnote*, won the Alice James Books New England and New York competition and was published in 1998. Her poetry has appeared in *The Paris Review, Ms., American Letters & Commentary, Denver Quarterly Review, Interim,* and in many other journals. She is the recipient of numerous awards and honors, including a grant-in-progress from the Vogelstein Foundation for *The Glazier's Country.* She lives in Brooklyn, New York.